Frog and Toad Are Friends
Frog and Toad Together
Frog and Toad All Year

by
Arnold Lobel

Teacher Guide

Written by
Phyllis A. Green

Note

The Harper Trophy paperback editions of the books were used to prepare this guide. The page references may differ in the hardcover or other paperback editions.

Please note: Please assess the appropriateness of these books for the age level and maturity of your students prior to reading and discussing it with your class.

ISBN 1-56137-207-2

Printed in the United States of America.

To order, contact your local school supply store, or—

Novel Units, Inc.
P.O. Box 433
Bulverde, TX 78163-0433

Web site: www.educyberstor.com

Table of Contents

Skills and Strategies

Thinking
Brainstorming, sorting

Vocabulary
Synonyms, antonyms, word mapping

Writing
Description, letter-writing, creative writing, pattern-writing

Comprehension
Comparison/contrast, predicting

Literary Elements
Characterization, story elements

Listening/Speaking
Interviewing, drama, interactive gestures

Organization of the Novel Unit

These three short books of sixty-four pages apiece are grouped together. They can provide an interesting unit of study of about three weeks duration. Each book has five stories in it, and presenting one story a day would fill fifteen days. In a three-week unit, you might want to change the pace with one of the stories to be read aloud or at home with parents. At the start, it is suggested that you provide a motivating initiating activity of set-up for the unit. A concluding celebration activity is in order.

Summary of the Books

Frog and Toad Are Friends, a Caldecott Honor Book, introduces two charming friends, Frog and Toad. They lack surnames but share characteristics of adults, children, humans, and animals. They each live in a separate human-like house and meet for friendly child-like encounters. From the book, students learn about friendship, frogs and toads, and how pleasant simple, straightforward expression is. In "Spring," Frog tricks (or convinces) Toad awake from his winter sleep by tearing off pages from his calendar, thereby tricking him into thinking spring has arrived. Toad finds Frog sick in "The Story." Toad ministers to his friend, who looks "quite green," with tea and comfort, but is unable to entertain Frog with a story. "A Lost Button" tells about Toad's loss of a button from his jacket. Toad is humorous in "A Swim" when he dons his bathing suit. In "The Letter," Frog sends Toad a letter via a slow-moving snail.

Frog and Toad Together, a Newbery Honor Book, is one of the series "An I Can Read Book." "A List," the first story in the book, details Frog's antics in reducing his life to a list. "The Garden" tells of Toad's efforts to grow a garden. "Cookies" has an odd turn of thought on cookies and will power: Frog and Toad offer the tempting cookies to the birds to help bolster their will power. In "Dragons and Giants," Frog and Toad feel very brave together after reading a suggestible book. In "The Dream," Toad dreams about being the greatest toad in all the world. However, in Toad's ascendency, Frog shrinks and shrinks. Toad is happy to awaken and share, as a normal-sized toad, a fine, long day with a normal-sized frog.

Frog and Toad All Year starts with "Down the Hill." In that story, Frog and Toad go sledding. In "The Corner," Frog tells Toad about growing into a frog from a polliwog. Frog and Toad rediscover spring. Toad tries unsuccessfully to bring home two chocolate ice cream cones in "Ice Cream." "The Surprise" tells of Frog and Toad surprising each other by raking leaves for their friend. "Christmas Eve" is a pleasant closing story about Toad's worry for his tardy friend, Frog.

Initiating Activities

Several possibilities are provided from which the teacher may choose.

1. For several days prior to starting the unit, display signs proclaiming, "The amphibians are coming!" When students ask, let them make guesses, perhaps recording the guesses on butcher block paper to return to later to prove or disprove.

2. Discuss friendship, a major theme of these books. Record answers on an attribute web. (See sample included with sample prompt questions and answers on page 9 of this guide.)

3. Complete a K-W-L chart with the students about frogs and toads. (See sample included on page 7 of this guide.)

   Display the K-W-L (on butcher block paper) in the classroom to revisit and complete later.

4. Distribute the frog and toad graphics page for students to color. (See pages 13 and 14 of this guide.) Then ask students why they were distributed.

5. Use an opaque projector to enlarge some of the graphics onto a large mural-sized piece of butcher block paper. Let students decorate the class mural as the unit unfolds.

6. Visit a nearby pond to observe frogs or toads.

Curricular Integration Possibilities Offered by the Frog and Toad Books
Science: Amphibians, pond life, class frog or toad "pet," seasons, environmental impacts, etc.

Graphic Organizers

These should be modeled by the teacher with class participation. A variety of possible answers should be listed by the teacher either on large sheets of paper or the blackboard. Only then should the children be asked to develop their own graphics. Children are encouraged to express their opinions, and to state what they know about a topic. The teacher lists these opinions and "facts" and later, as the children read and discover that some of their ideas are incorrect, these ideas may be crossed out on the large sheets. Students should be encouraged to elaborate on their answers, justify their opinions, prove their predictions, and relate what they have read to their lives.

T-charts show likenesses and differences of two characters, plots, setting, etc.

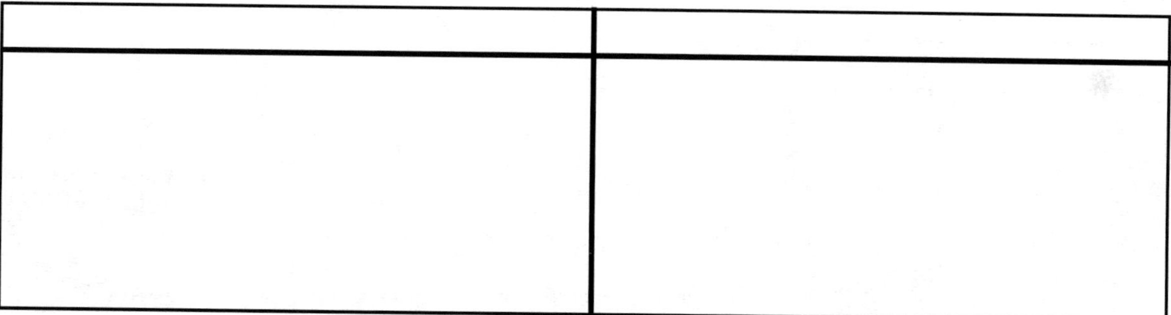

Venn diagrams are taken from math in which characteristics of two characters are listed and the overlap or similarity can be seen.

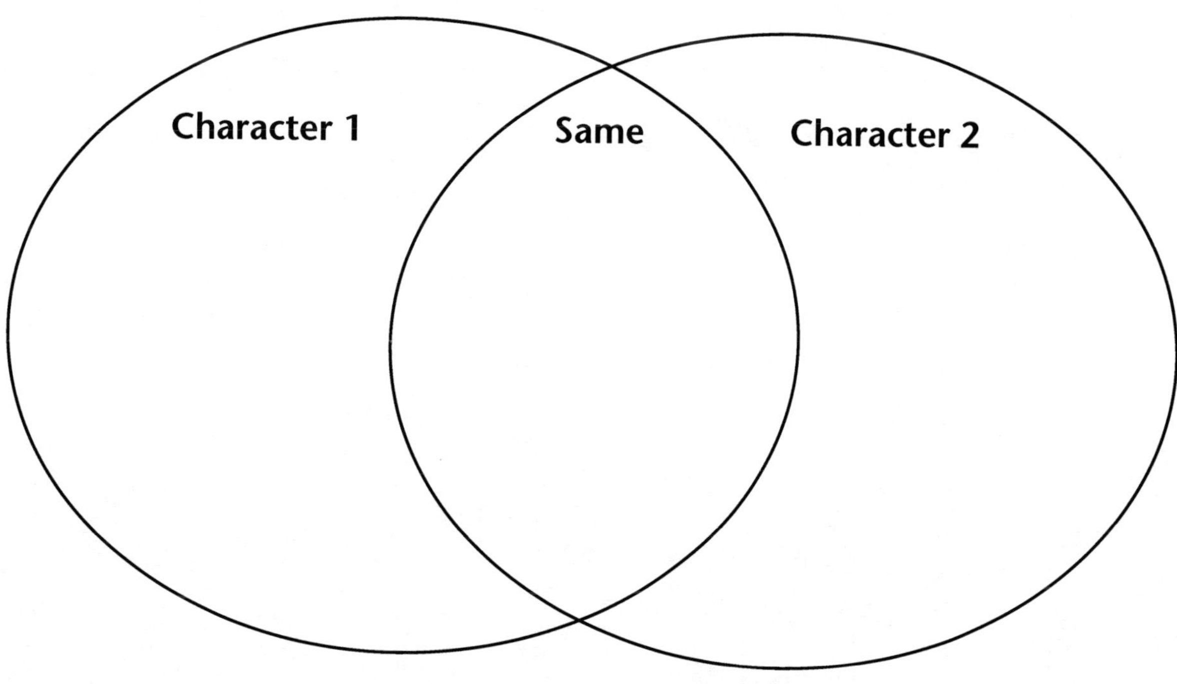

Using Predictions in the Novel Unit Approach

We all make predictions as we read—little guesses about what will happen next, how the conflict will be resolved, which details given by the author will be important to the plot, which details will help to fill in our sense of a character. Students should be encouraged to predict, to make sensible guesses. As students work on predictions, these discussion questions can be used to guide them: What are some of the ways to predict? What is the process of a sophisticated reader's thinking and predicting? What clues does an author give us to help us in making our predictions? Why are some predictions more likely than others?

A predicting chart is for students to record their predictions. As each subsequent chapter is discussed, you can review and correct previous predictions. This procedure serves to focus on predictions and to review the stories.

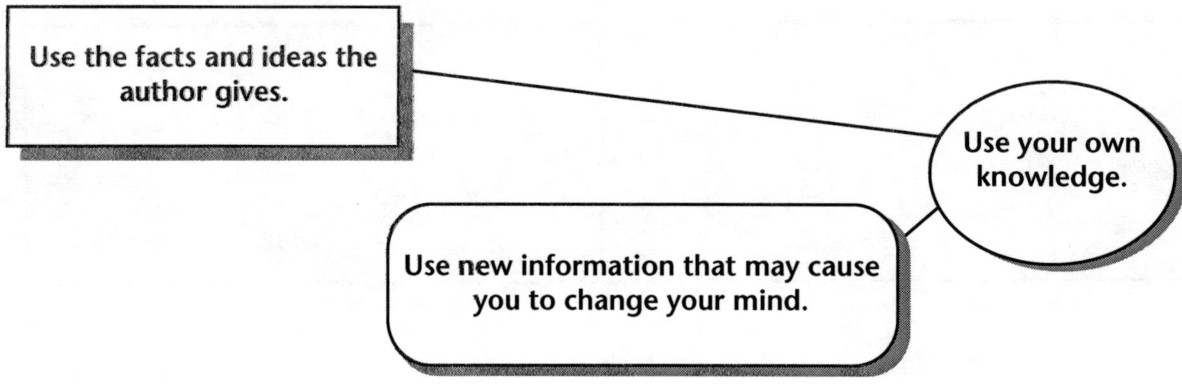

Prediction Chart

What characters have we met so far?	What is the conflict in the story?	What are your predictions?	Why did you make those predictions?

K-L-W Chart

What They Know	What They Would Like to Know	What They Learned

Story Map

Setting
Problem
Goal
Episodes
Resolution
Characters
Time and Place
Beginning
Development
Outcome

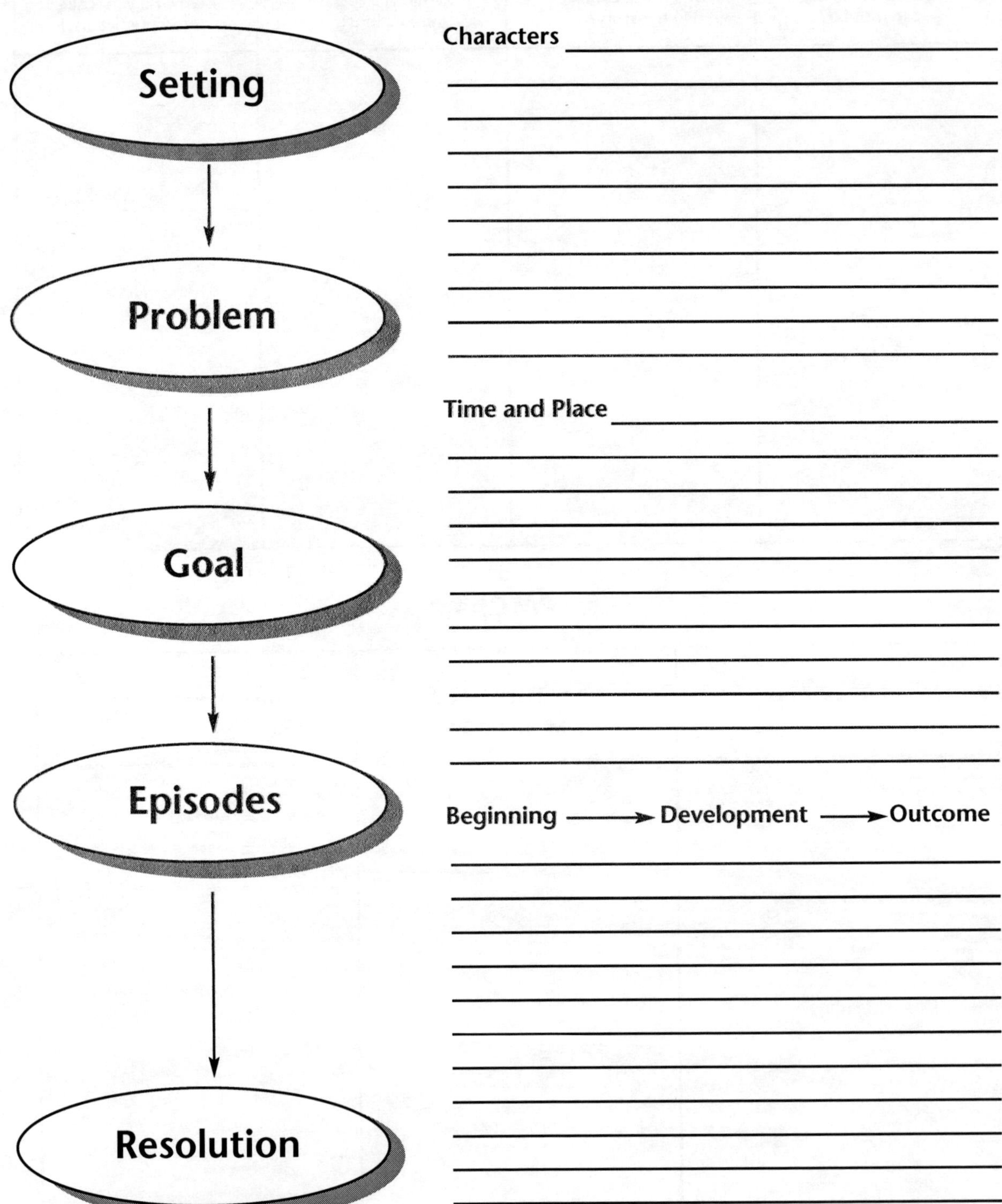

Using Attribute Webs in the Novel Unit Approach

Attribute Webs are simply a visual representation of a character from the novel. They provide a systematic way for the students to organize and recap the information they have about a particular character. Attribute webs may be used after reading the novel to recapitulate information about a particular character or completed gradually as information unfolds, done individually, or finished as a group project.

One type of character attribute web uses these divisions:

- How a character acts and feels. (How does the character feel in this picture? How would you feel if this happened to you? How do you think the character feels?)
- How a character looks. (Close your eyes and picture the character. Describe him to me.)
- Where a character lives. (Where and when does the character live?)
- How others feel about the character. (How does another specific character feel about our character?)

In group discussion about the student attribute webs and specific characters, the teacher can ask for backup proof from the novel. You can also include inferential thinking.

Attribute webs need not be confined to characters. They may also be used to organize information about a word, concept, object or place. See the example below.

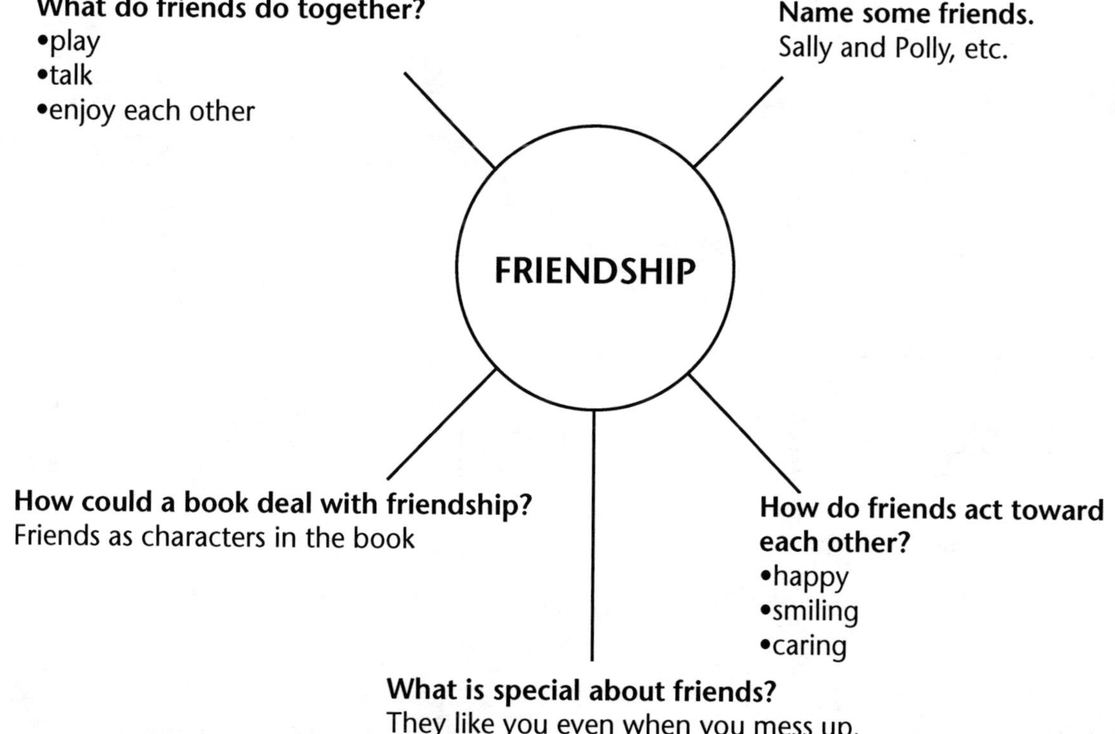

Character Attribute Web

The attribute web below is designed to help you gather clues the author provides about what a character is like. Fill in the blanks with words and phrases which tell how the character acts and looks, as well as what the character says and what others say about him or her.

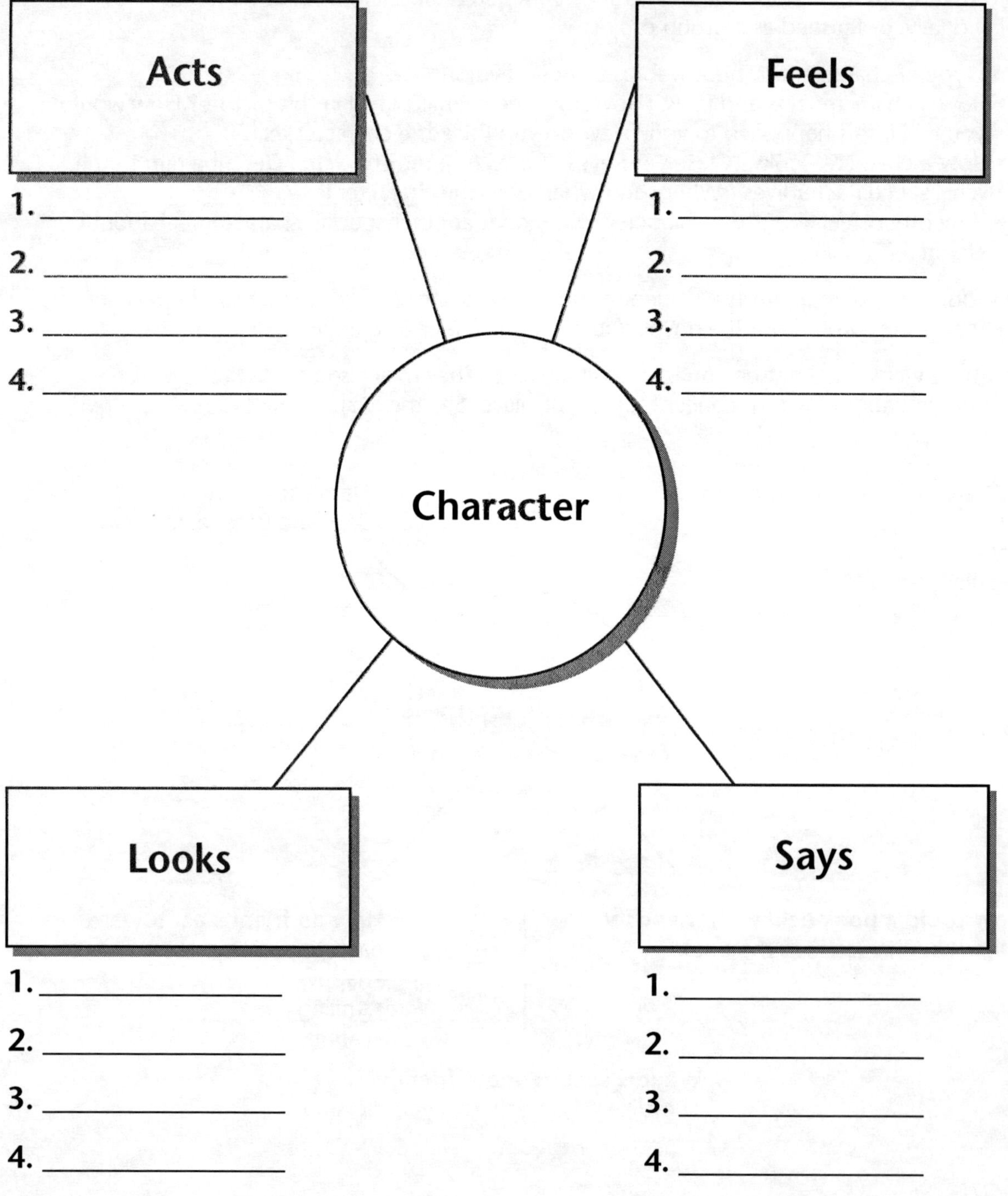

Reproducible Graphics

Background Information on Frogs and Toads

Frogs and toads are amphibians; i.e., they live their early lives in water, breathing through gills, but develop lungs as they grow older so they can breathe air and live on land. Frog and toad eggs hatch as tadpoles, funny-looking creatures which look a lot like fish. Frogs and toads look quite a bit alike, but most frogs are smooth, long, and graceful, while most toads are dry, warty, and squat. Most frogs have teeth while most toads do not.

Frogs usually live on the banks of streams and ponds. Toads usually live on land, digging out caves where they are found during the day. They come out at twilight to feed. Both are insect-eaters, catching their food on their sticky tongues. Frogs and toads are cold-blooded.

Frogs and toads hibernate in winter, burying themselves in mud or caves where they stay all winter. Cold-blooded, they become very cold hibernating and require little oxygen because they are burning little food. Both species often change their skin, slipping the old one off over their heads.

Comparison Chart

Frogs	Toads	Both
• smooth, slippery, graceful • usually live on banks of streams and ponds • vary considerably in shape, color, and size • bullfrog, leopard frog, and wood frog the most common in the U.S.	• dry, warty, squat • usually live on land • those living in temperate regions are usually brown and olive • those living in the tropics are frequently brightly colored	• amphibians • cold-blooded • hibernate • insect-eaters

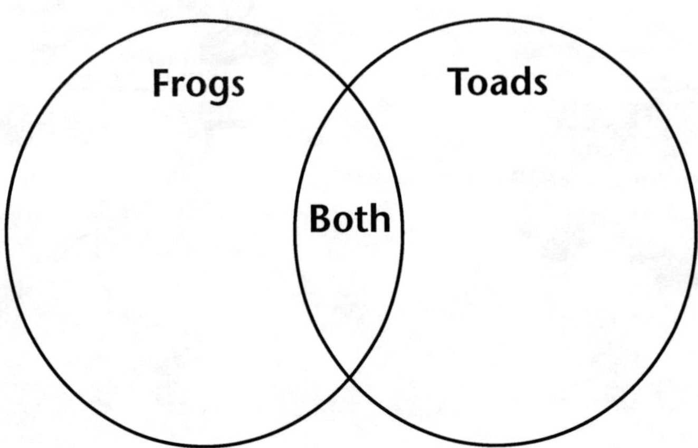

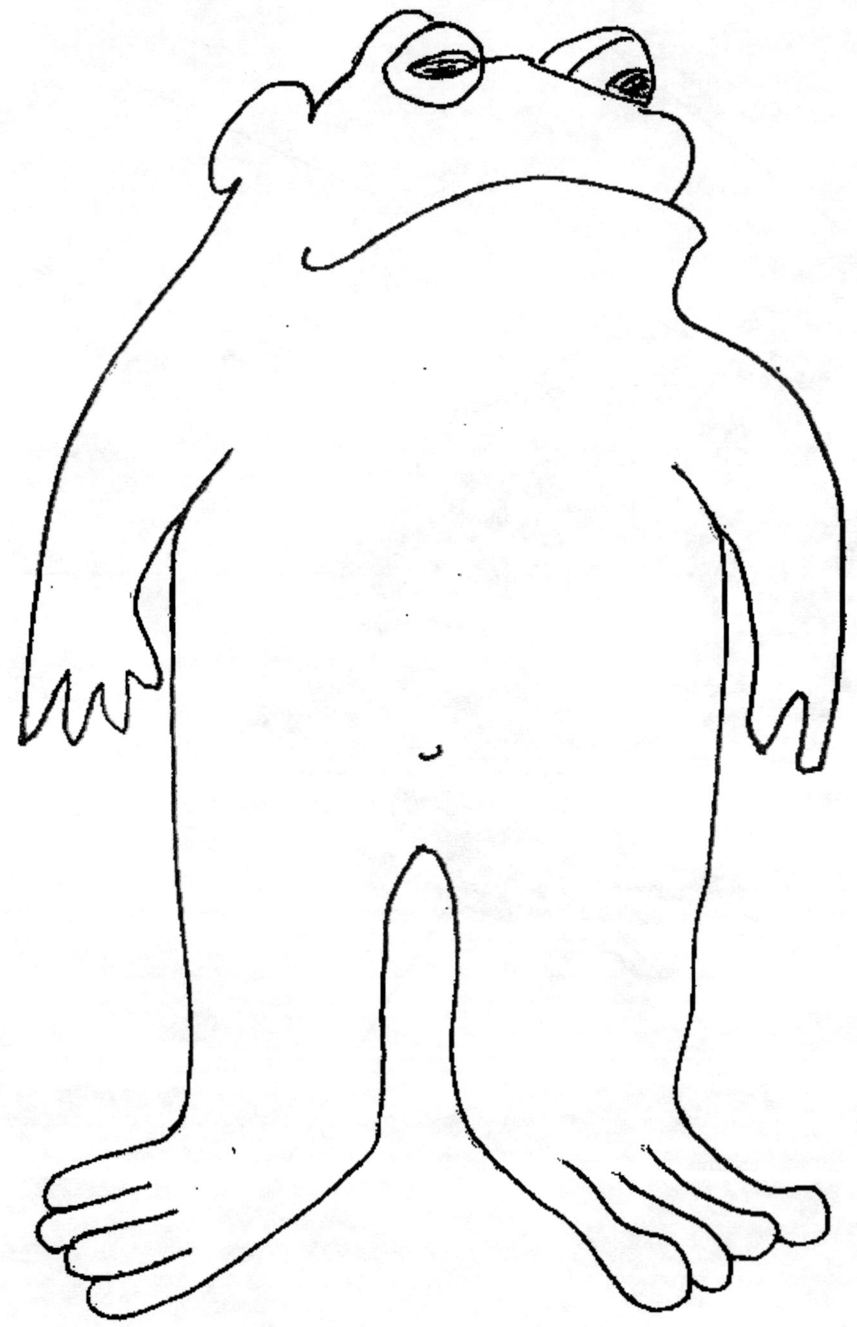

Chapter-by-Chapter
Vocabulary, Discussion Questions, and Activities

Frog and Toad Are Friends — "Spring"

Vocabulary

path 4	knocked 4	voice 4	inside 4
shining 5	melting 5	shutters 6	lying 6
covers 7	blinked 7	meadows 8	evenings 8
porch 8	calendar 14	outside 15	

Motivation

The title of the story is "Spring." Look at the picture on page 5. Does it look like spring? Why or why not? Make some guesses about the story.

Discussion Questions

1. Why is Toad sleeping when Frog knocks on his front door? (*Page 6, He is taking a long winter's nap—hibernating. Hibernation: spending the winter in close quarters in a dormant [sleeping] state*)
2. What fun does Frog expect in the spring? (*page 8, "clear warm light," skipping through the meadows, running through the woods, swimming in the river, counting stars)*
3. What is a meadow? (*grassland*) What are some words you might use instead of meadow? (*Answers will vary—field, pasture, hayfield.*)
4. Compare your spring activities and those activities Frog describes. *(Frog: skipping in meadows, swimming in river, counting stars. You: baseball, soccer, planting garden. Answers will vary.)* Why the difference? (*Answers will vary.*)
5. How does Frog trick (or convince) Toad into thinking spring has come? (*pages 13-14, by tearing off months from Toad's calendar*)
6. How do you think Toad felt waking up early? (*Answers will vary.*) How do you feel if you are awakened early? (*Answers will vary.*)

Supplementary Activities

1. Start attribute webs for Toad and Frog, noting what the author has revealed about them thus far. Students can have individual webs (sample included suitable for duplication) to go along with a class web. Keep adding to the webs as the unit proceeds. (See page 10 of this guide.)
2. Draw two pictures on a divided piece of paper. On one side draw Toad sleeping and on the other side draw you sleeping. How are you alike? How are you different?

Frog and Toad Are Friends

"The Story"

Vocabulary

summer 16	thought 18	perhaps 19	poured 22
bang 24	against 24	anymore 25	because 25
terrible 25	answer 27		

Motivation

What is your favorite story? Allow students to think briefly and then share with a partner. A few might share with the whole class. The teacher could share her own favorite story. Announce that Toad in our next selection tries to think of a story.

Discussion Questions

1. Why is Frog looking quite green? (*Page 16, He is sick.*) Why is saying, "Frog, you are looking quite green" funny? (*Frogs are usually green. This is an application of a human expression to an animal.*)
2. How does Toad take care of his sick friend? (*Pages 16-17, He gets him to bed and makes him a cup of hot tea.*)
3. What is the problem about the story? (*Toad can't think of a story to tell Frog.*)
4. What does Toad do to try to think of a story? (*pages 18-23, He thinks and thinks, walks up and down on the porch, stands on his head, pours a glass of water over his head, and bangs his head against a wall.*)
5. Are Toad's ways to think of a story good? Why or why not? (*Answers will vary.*)
6. What is funny about Frog's story? (*Page 26, He tells about Toad thinking of a story.*)

Supplementary Activities

1. Act out the story. Class members think of motions for the parts of the story, practice, and then act out as the teacher or a classmate reads the story aloud.
2. Conduct a survey about favorite stories. The class decides upon categories for stories (e.g., animal, scary, friends, etc.) which are written (and given a graphic reminder) on a large chart or the chalkboard. Students "vote" for one category. Afterwards, students tally the results and make a graph.
3. What are some funny or different ways to describe being sick? Brainstorm and record answers. Students can then decorate the "sick poster." *(green around the gills, looking quite green, a bit off, not up to par, pale, feeling under the weather, looking peaked, ill, having a bug)*
4. Complete a story map about the story. (See page 8 of this guide.)

"A Lost Button"

Vocabulary

meadow 28	drat 28	buttons 29	jacket 29
worry 30	sparrow 32	raccoon 34	screamed 36
slammed 37	trouble 37	shelf 38	

Motivation

Complete a button web or brainstorm to think of all different kinds of buttons. Then announce that today's story is called "A Lost Button."

Discussion Questions

1. What are Toad's two complaints after a long walk with Frog? (*Page 29, His feet hurt and he has lost a button from his jacket.*)
2. What is Frog's solution for Toad? (*page 30, retrace their walk to find the lost button*)
3. How does Frog and Toad's search for the button turn out? (*Pages 31-36, Toad finds and is given a lot of different buttons, none matching those on his jacket.*)
4. Does Toad ever find his lost button? (*page 37, yes*) Where? (*page 37, at home*)
5. What does Toad do with all the other buttons? (*Page 38, He sews them all over his jacket.*)

Supplementary Activities

1. Design your own button and draw a picture of it. On a separate piece of paper, write a description of it. Display the button pictures and let students read the descriptions and try to match with the illustrations.
2. Grandma's Button Box: Collect a lot of different buttons. Spill out a few and ask students to sort them into groups. Students choose and explain the groups (e.g., 2-holed, 4-holed, shank, shiny, white, colored, fabric, ugly, pretty, children's, shirt).
3. Duplicate the sheet included for students to decorate their own jackets. (See page 31 of this guide.)

Frog and Toad Are Friends "A Swim"

Vocabulary

bathing 40	splashes 43	riverbank 44	lizards 46
dragonflies 47	field mouse 47	shiver 49	sneeze 49

Motivation

"How do you get ready to go swimming?" Ask students to answer, brainstorming and recording answers on the chalkboard. Then announce that Toad and Frog will also get ready to swim in the next story, "A Swim."

Discussion Questions

1. How are Frog and Toad different as they get ready to go for a swim? (*Page 40, Toad wears a bathing suit, but Frog doesn't.*)

2. Why doesn't Toad want Frog to see his bathing suit? (*page 42, because he looks funny in the bathing suit*)

3. Why does Frog swim fast and make big splashes, while Toad swims slowly and makes smaller splashes? (*Page 43, They are two different kinds of animals.*)

4. What do the lizards, dragonflies, snake, and field mouse do when Frog tells them to go away? (*Pages 46-47, They gather on the riverbank to see Toad in his bathing suit.*)

5. Why does Toad finally come out of the water? (*Page 49, He is getting too cold to stay in the water.*)

Supplementary Activities

1. Duplicate the bathing suit sheet included for students to design bathing suits for the animals. (See page 33 of this guide.)

2. Check the attribute webs for Toad and Frog, adding more descriptions.

3. Prepare a T-comparison chart of the characters Toad and Frog. On one side, list their animal characteristics; on the other side, list their human characteristics. *(Animal-Like: look like toads and frogs, hibernate; Human-Like: talk, wear clothes)*

Frog and Toad Are Friends "The Letter"

Vocabulary

mail 54	mailbox 55	hurried 56	pencil 56
envelope 57	snail 57	waiting 58	because 61
together 63	pleased 64		

Motivation

Dramatically open a green envelope (if you can find one) and remove a letter written on green paper. Read this letter to the class:

Dear Students,

We are happy that you are reading about us. We have a lot of fun being friends. Please write to us soon.

Love,
Frog and Toad

Announce that the next story is about "The Letter."

Discussion Questions

1. Why does Toad feel sad? (*page 54, because he never gets any mail*)

2. How does Frog decide to cheer up his friend Toad? (*Page 57, He sends him a letter.*)

3. Why do Frog and Toad wait so long for the letter? (*page 64, because Frog sent the letter with a snail*)

Supplementary Activities

1. Duplicate the snail as mail carrier sheet. Students design a uniform for the snail as a mail carrier. (See page 32 of this guide.)

2. Write letters to Frog and Toad.

Frog and Toad Together "A List"

Vocabulary

list 4	remember 4	crossed 5	something 7
closet 8	knocked 10	swamps 15	

Motivation

Let's make a list of things we're doing today at school ("A list of things to do today"). We'll cross items off as we do them. Today's Frog and Toad story is called "A List."

Discussion Questions

1. Why do you think Toad wants to make a list? (*page 4, to help him remember the many things he wants to do that day*)

2. How does Toad use his list? (*Pages 5-12, He crosses off items as he does them.*)

3. Why does Toad call for help? (*Pages 13-14, His list blows away but he can't run and catch it because running after his list isn't on the list.*)

4. Is Toad silly about his list? Why?

Supplementary Activities

1. Make your own list, maybe for what to do after school.

2. Analysis: What are pluses and minuses to lists? *(Pluses: helps you remember, helps you be organized; Minuses: may restrict you, you may not need the list.)*

3. Interview an adult about lists.

4. Look at the illustrations in the book. What colors does Arnold Lobel use? Why?

5. Take out a green, brown, and a black crayon. Draw a Frog and Toad illustration.

Frog and Toad Together

"The Garden"

Vocabulary

garden 18	seeds 18	ground 18	afraid 22
	candles 24	frightened 27	

Motivation

Show students either seed catalogs or some proceeds from a garden. Ask what clues these items can give you about today's Frog and Toad story.

Discussion Questions

1. Why does Toad decide to plant a garden? (*Page 18, Toad admires Frog's garden and wants to plant one himself.*)
2. What funny things does Toad do to get his garden to grow? (*pages 20-26, shouts at them, puts out candles because he thinks they are afraid of the dark, reads the seeds a story, sings songs to the seeds, reads poems to the seeds, plays music to the seeds*)
3. Why does Toad think his seeds finally grow? (*Page 29, Toad thinks his seeds finally stop being afraid to grow.*) Is Toad's thinking correct? Why or why not?
4. How are Frog and Toad different about gardening? (*Frog plants a garden in the usual way; Toad thinks of his plant seeds as "human-like" children.*) Continue this thinking with a comparison of Frog and Toad.

Frog	Toad
• helps his friend • supportive • leader • green	• often has silly, funny ideas (list, bathing suit) • follower • brown

Supplementary Activities

1. Brainstorm ideas about "nurturing," "mothering," and "parenting," taking care of seeds or children.

What Seeds Need	What Children Need
• light • water • nutrients	• attention • soothing of their fears • food (nutrients) • exposure to "good things" (poems, music)

2. Using several sheets of paper, illustrate the various scenes in the story, perhaps assigning various scenes to individual students or groups. Tape the sheets together in order to make a long mural, or roll the sheets up and make a "TV" roll which can be "played" back as the story is reread.

Vocabulary

cookies 30	taste 30	will power 34	string 39
everywhere 40	beaks 40		

Motivation

The teacher dramatically describes her own favorite cookies, building excitement for the children. Ask for some limited sharing about cookies, and then announce that Frog and Toad deal with cookies in today's story.

Discussion Questions

1. What is Frog's reaction to Toad's cookies? (*Page 31, Frog says they are the best cookies he's ever eaten.*)
2. Would you eat as many cookies as Frog and Toad? Why or why not? (*Answers will vary.*)
3. What is Frog's definition of will power? (*page 35, trying hard not to do something you really want to do*)
4. What is Frog's first idea to help Toad and him to stop eating all the cookies? (*page 36, put the cookies in a box*)
5. What are the additions that Frog and Toad make with the box to help with their will power? (*Pages 37-39, They add string around the box and put the box on a high shelf.*)
6. How does Frog finally solve the cookie problem? (*Page 40, He opens the box and calls the birds, who pick up all the cookies and fly away.*)
7. How does the story end? (*Page 41, Toad says he is going home to bake a cake.*) Why is that funny? (*Answers will vary.*)

Supplementary Activities

1. Analysis: What is will power? Discuss times you've needed will power or your parents have wanted will power. Compare the ways Frog and Toad try to increase their will power with the ideas you have.

Frog and Toad	Me
• put the cookies out of sight • make them hard to get • give the temptation (cookies) away	• do something else • ask parents or someone else for help

2. Writing: What do you think the birds think about the cookies?

Frog and Toad Together

"Dragons and Giants"

Vocabulary

dragons 42	giants 42	mirror 42	brave 43
outside 44	mountain 44	cave 45	shaking 45
avalanche 46	trembling 47	shadow 48	hawk 48

Motivation

"Have you ever been afraid? How does it feel?" Brainstorm some answers with the class. Then announce that in today's story, Frog and Toad are afraid.

Discussion Questions

1. Why do Frog and Toad wonder if they are brave? (*Page 42, They just read a book about brave people who fight dragons and giants.*)
2. Make a list of Frog and Toad's adventures, checking on their bravery. After each adventure is listed on the chalkboard or butcher block paper, ask students for predictions about what will happen next.

Adventures in Search of Bravery

- climb a mountain (page 44)
- see a snake come out of a dark cave (page 45)
- run away from an avalanche (pages 46-47)
- see the shadow of a hawk (page 48)

3. Why is the shadow of the hawk scary? (*Hawks prey on small animals and might eat Frog and Toad.*)
4. Where do Frog and Toad go at the end of the story? (*Page 50, Toad hides in bed under the covers and Frog jumps into the closet.*)
5. Are Frog and Toad brave?

Supplementary Activities

1. Dramatics: Act out the story with hand motions for each of the adventures. All students practice the motions and then go through them as the teacher rereads the story. (The listing from the "Discussion Questions" may help.)
2. Art: Draw a picture of yourself or a friend being brave on one side of a piece of paper, and feeling safe (like Frog and Toad at the end of the story) on the other side.

Frog and Toad Together — "The Dream"

Vocabulary

dream 52	costume 52	bow 54	high wire 56
peeped 57	wonderful 59	theater 59	

Motivation

"Close your eyes and imagine you are Toad and are dreaming about being the greatest toad in all the world. How do you feel?"

Discussion Questions

1. Where does the story take place? Set the scene. (*Page 52, Toad is on a stage in costume and Frog is sitting in the theater.*)

2. What is the first thing Toad does on stage? (*page 54, play the piano*)

3. How does Toad treat Frog afterwards? (*Page 55, Toad asks Frog if he can play the piano like Toad.*)

4. How does that make Frog feel? (*page 55, smaller and smaller*)

5. How does Toad's dream end? (*Page 60, Frog is very, very small and Toad is looking for him and calling for him to come back.*)

6. How does the story end? (*Page 64, Toad wakes up with new appreciation of Frog as a friend.*)

Supplementary Activity

Writing: Finish these sentences:

A friend is ____

Frog and Toad are friends because ______________________________

____

Frog and Toad All Year

"Down the Hill"

Vocabulary

beautiful 4	brought 6	snowpants 6	tramped 8
sled 8	rushed 10	leaped 11	snowbank 11
steer 11			

Motivation

Frog says, "Winter is beautiful." Do you agree? How can winter be beautiful? Discuss with the class.

Discussion Questions

1. What winter clothes does Frog bring for Toad to wear? (*pages 6-7, coat, snowpants, hat, scarf*)
2. What is Toad's reaction to the winter clothes? (*Page 7, He doesn't like them.*)
3. What happens to Toad on the sled? (*Pages 10-12, After Frog falls off, Toad at first has a wonderful time.*)
4. How does Toad's ride change after he talks to Crow? (*Pages 13-15, He realizes he is alone and the sled hits a tree, hits a rock, and dives into the snow.*)
5. How do you think Toad feels when he discovers he is alone? (*Answers will vary.*)
6. Compare Frog and Toad in this story.

Frog	Toad
• loves winter outdoors • likes sledding • leads	• wants to stay in bed • is scared alone on the sled • follows along

Supplementary Activities

1. Analysis: Why do you need winter clothes? Compare the environment in the different seasons for your home on a chart.

Winter	Spring	Summer	Fall
• cold • snow (wet) • wind	• rain • temperature varies • lengthening days	• hot • long days	• temperature varies • shorter days

2. Use the frog graphics page. (See pages 13 and 14 of this guide.) Ask students to provide winter clothes for the frogs and toads.

Vocabulary

spoiled 18	stove 18	polliwog 20	corner 21
pebbles 22	stump 23	lizard 25	outside 28

Motivation

Write on the chalkboard: Spring, Corner, Father Frog, and Son Frog. These words are important in this story. Let's make some predictions (guesses) about the story.

Discussion Questions

1. Why does Toad think the day is spoiled? (*page 18, because he is all wet from being caught in the rain*)

2. Does Frog understand his father when his father says spring is just around the corner? (*Page 21, No. Frog thinks of a physical, actual corner.*)

3. Where does Frog search for the corner? (*pages 21-24, on a path in the woods, in a meadow, along a river*)

4. Once Frog comes home tired, what signs of spring does he find? (*page 27, birds singing, flowers in the garden, mother and father working in the garden*)

5. Look at the picture on page 31. Did Frog and Toad find spring around the corner? Why? Give reasons for your answer.

Supplementary Activities

1. Make a list of phrases which can be misunderstood, like "spring is just around the corner" or "it's raining cats and dogs." Brainstorm a list and then allow individual students to choose one to illustrate in a humorous way.

2. Make a spring list using each letter of the word as a descriptor.

   S — sunny
   P —
   R — rain
   I —
   N —
   G —

Frog and Toad All Year — "Ice Cream"

Vocabulary

summer 30	licked 31	chocolate 31	splattered 34
awful 36	heavens 39	bottom 40	

Motivation

"Close your eyes and imagine eating your favorite ice cream cone."

Discussion Questions

1. Why does Toad go to buy ice cream cones? (*Page 30, Frog thinks they will taste good.*)
2. What do you predict may cause Toad trouble with the cones? (*Answers will vary.*)
3. What happens to Toad and the cones? (*Pages 32-39, The ice cream melts and Toad is covered with sticks and leaves.*)
4. How do the mouse, squirrel, and rabbit react to Toad with ice cream? (*Pages 36-37, They don't recognize him and are scared.*)
5. What's the better way that Frog and Toad get their ice cream? (*Page 41, They both go to a store and sit under a tree to eat.*)

Supplementary Activities

1. Writing: Why do we think of ice cream with summer? Write a short answer. Share your answer with a partner.
2. Mathematics: Conduct a class survey about favorite ice cream flavors. Then make a graph.
3. Writing: Why is your favorite ice cream flavor your favorite? Explain in a short paragraph.

Vocabulary

surprised 42 rake 43 shed 43 messy 44
pleased 44

Motivation

Hold up some fall leaves or show pictures of fall leaves. What's special about fall leaves? What job do we have in fall?

Discussion Questions

1. What is the surprise Frog plans for Toad? (*page 42, raking his lawn*)
2. What is the surprise Toad plans for Frog? (*page 44, raking his lawn*)
3. What happens to the leaves that have been raked up? (*Pages 50-52, The leaves blow back both on Frog's and Toad's lawns.*)
4. What should Frog and Toad have done with the leaves? (*Answers will vary.*)
5. Why is "The Surprise" a funny story? (*Answers will vary.*)

Supplementary Activities

1. Writing: Complete these sentences:

   My favorite surprise was ____

   ____.

   I'd like to surprise ____

   ____.

2. Discussion or Group Work: Each group receives a blank attribute web with surprise in the middle to complete.

Frog and Toad All Year

"Christmas Eve"

Vocabulary

decorated 54	worried 55	terrible 56	hungry 57
cellar 59	lantern 59	attic 59	frying pan 60
wrapping 62			

Motivation

Look at the picture on page 55. What do you see in the picture? Make some predictions about the story from the title and the picture.

Discussion Questions

1. How do you feel when someone is late? (*Answers will vary.*) Who is late in the story? (*page 54, Frog*) Does Toad react the same way you do? Explain.

2. As time passes, what does Toad imagine has happened to Frog? (*pages 56-58, that he has fallen into a deep hole, is lost in the woods, is cold and wet and hungry, is being chased by a big animal*)

3. What does Toad take with him to help Frog? (*pages 59-60, rope, lantern, frying pan*)

4. Who does Toad meet as he runs out of his house? (*page 62, Frog*)

5. How does the story end? (*Page 64, Toad and Frog have a nice Christmas Eve, and Toad likes his present, a beautiful new clock.*)

Supplementary Activities

1. Toad asks a lot of "What if..." questions in this story. Find those questions in the story. Make up three more "What if..." questions to share with your classmates.

2. What would you take to rescue someone who was late to a party?

Concluding Activities

1. Frog and Toad have different human-like feelings in the various stories. Fill in this chart for each of the stories.

Story	Feeling
Spring	
The Story	
A Lost Button	
A Swim	
The Letter	
A List	
The Garden	
Cookies	
Dragons and Giants	
The Dream	
Down the Hill	
The Corner	
Ice Cream	
The Surprise	
Christmas Eve	

2. Rate these books. Why do you like them? Which is the best? What is the best story? Why? Explain your answers.

3. Review your attribute webs to add or remove information about Frog and Toad.

NAME: ____

Directions
Decorate your jacket.

NAME: ____________________

Directions
Create a uniform for a snail mail carrier.

NAME: ____

Directions
Create bathing suits for these animals who laughed at Toad.

Frog and Toad Friendship Notes

Students are encouraged to share friendship notes at the end of the day, putting them in classmates' mailboxes. The teacher can also participate. The teacher duplicates these forms on green paper for students to use.

TO: ______________________________

FROM: Your Frog and Toad Classmate

You're my friend today because ______________________________

Vocabulary Activities

1. Use the wheel to work with each of the vocabulary words.

2. Collect on a bulletin board or chart pictures of frogs, toads, and other images suggested by the stories. Add labels.

3. Make up sentences using the vocabulary words to display on a word wall. Write the sentences on sentence strips, using a line for the vocabulary word. Students try to fill in the blanks, either alone or with partners.

4. Map some of the words.

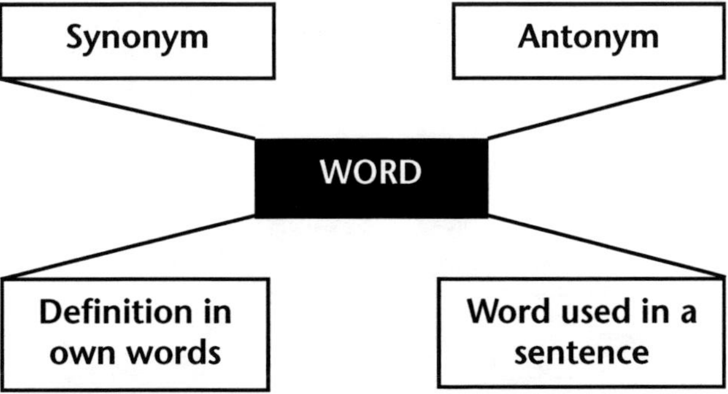

5. Create synonym chains with some of the words.
   decorated—adorned—
   splashes—
   screamed—yelled—shouted—

Assessment for the Frog and Toad Books

Overview

Assessment is an on-going process. The following ten items can be completed during the novel study. Points may be added to indicate the level of understanding. Once completed, the student and teacher will check them.

Student	Teacher	
________	________	1. Create a K-W-L chart about frogs and toads.
________	________	2. Keep making predictions as you read each story. Record on a chart.
________	________	3. What did you learn about friendship from the book? Answer orally, in writing, or with pictures.
________	________	4. Keep webs about Frog and Toad.
________	________	5. Fill in a story map about two of the stories.
________	________	6. Do two comparison T-charts.
________	________	7. Dramatize a favorite Frog and Toad story.
________	________	8. Write a letter to Frog or Toad.
________	________	9. Finish the Frog and Toad charts on page 22 of this guide.
________	________	10. Vote for your favorite Frog and Toad story. Give reasons for your choice.